The Great Fire of London

Samuel Pepys

A Phoenix Paperback

This abridgement contains pages 267 to 306 from Volume III of
The Diary of Samuel Pepys

This edition first published in 1996 by Phoenix
a division of Orion Books Ltd
Orion House, 5 Upper St Martin's Lane, London WC2H 9EA

ISBN 1 85799 521 X

Typeset by Deltatype Ltd, Ellesmere Port, Cheshire
Printed in Great Britain by Clays Ltd, St Ives plc.

THE GREAT FIRE
OF LONDON

September 1666

1 September 1666

My wife and I to Polichinello, but were there horribly frighted to see Young Killigrew come in, with a great many more young sparks: but we hid ourselves, so as we think they did not see us.

2 September 1666

(Lord's day.) Some of our maids sitting up late last night to get things ready against our feast to-day, Jane called us up about three in the morning, to tell us of a great fire they saw in the City. So I rose, and slipped on my night-gown, and went to her window; and thought it to be on the back-side of Marke-lane at the farthest; but, being unused to such fires as followed, I thought it far enough off; and so went to bed again, and to sleep. About seven rose again to dress myself, and there looked out at the window, and saw the fire not so much as it was, and further off. So to my closet to set things to rights, after yesterday's cleaning. By and by Jane comes and tells me that she hears that above 300 houses have been burned down to-night by the fire we saw, and that it is now burning down all Fish Street, by London Bridge. So I made myself ready presently, and walked to the Tower; and there got up upon one of the high places, Sir J. Robinson's little son going up with me; and there I did see the houses at that end of the bridge all on fire, and an infinite great fire on this and the other side the end of the bridge; which, among other people, did trouble me for poor little Michell and our Sarah on the bridge. So down, with my heart full of trouble, to the Lieutenant of the Tower, who tells me that it begun this morning in the King's baker's* house in Pudding-lane, and that it hath burned down St. Magnus's Church and most part of Fish Street already. So I down to the water-side, and there got a boat, and through bridge, and there saw a lamentable fire. Poor Michell's house, as far as the Old Swan, already burned that way, and the fire running further, that, in a very little time, it got as far as the Steele-yard, while I was there. Every body endeavouring to remove their goods, and flinging into the river, or bringing them into lighters that lay off; poor people

4   * His name was Faryner.

staying in their houses as long as till the very fire touched them, and then running into boats, or clambering from one pair of stairs, by the waterside, to another. And, among other things, the poor pigeons, I perceive, were loth to leave their houses, but hovered about the windows and balconys, till they burned their wings, and fell down. Having staid, and in an hour's time seen the fire rage every way; and nobody, to my sight, endeavouring to quench it, but to remove their goods, and leave all to the fire; and, having seen it get as far as the Steeleyard, and the wind mighty high, and driving it into the City; and everything, after so long a drought, proving combustible, even the very stones of churches; and, among other things, the poor steeple* by which pretty Mrs—— lives, and whereof my old schoolfellow Elborough is parson, taken fire in the very top, and there burned till it fell down; I to White Hall, with a gentleman with me, who desired to go off from the Tower, to see the fire, in my boat; and there up to the King's closet in the Chapel, where people come about me, and I did give them an account dismayed them all, and word was carried in to the King. So I was called for,

* St Lawrence Poultney, of which Thomas Elborough was curate.

and did tell the King and Duke of York what I saw; and that, unless his Majesty did command houses to be pulled down, nothing could stop the fire. They seemed much troubled, and the King commanded me to go to my Lord Mayor* from him, and command him to spare no houses, but to pull down before the fire every way. The Duke of York bid me tell him, that if he would have any more soldiers, he shall; and so did my Lord Arlington afterwards, as a great secret. Here meeting with Captain Cocke, I in his coach, which he lent me, and Creed with me to Paul's; and there walked along Watling Street, as well as I could, every creature coming away loaden with goods to save, and, here and there, sick people carried away in beds. Extraordinary good goods carried in carts and on backs. At last met my Lord Mayor in Canning Street, like a man spent, with a handkercher about his neck. To the King's message, he cried, like a fainting woman, 'Lord! what can I do? I am spent: people will not obey me. I have been pulling down houses; but the fire overtakes us faster than we can do it.' That he needed no more soldiers; and that, for himself, he must go and refresh himself, having been up all night. So he left me, and I him, and walked home; seeing people

* Sir Thomas Bludworth.

all almost distracted, and no manner of means used to quench the fire. The houses, too, so very thick thereabouts, and full of matter for burning, as pitch and tar, in Thames Street; and warehouses of oyle, and wines, and brandy, and other things. Here I saw Mr Isaac Houblon, the handsome man, prettily dressed and dirty at his door at Dowgate, receiving some of his brother's things, whose houses were on fire; and, as he says, have been removed twice already; and he doubts, as it soon proved, that they must be, in a little time, removed from his house also, which was a sad consideration. And to see the churches all filling with goods by people who themselves should have been quietly there at this time. By this time, it was about twelve o'clock; and so home, and there find my guests, who were Mr Wood and his wife Barbary Shelden, and also Mr Moone: she mighty fine, and her husband, for aught I see, a likely man. But Mr Moone's design and mine, which was to look over my closet, and please him with the sight thereof, which he hath long desired, was wholly disappointed; for we were in great trouble and disturbance at this fire, not knowing what to think of it. However, we had an extraordinary good dinner, and as merry as at this time we could be. While at dinner, Mrs Batelier come to enquire after Mr Woolfe and Stanes, who, it seems, are related to them, whose houses in Fish Street are all burned, and they in a sad condition. She would not stay in the fright. Soon as dined, I and Moone away, and walked through the City, the streets full of nothing but people; and horses and carts loaden with goods, ready to run over one another, and removing goods from one burned house to another. They now removing out of Canning Street, which received goods in the morning, into Lumbard Street, and further: and, among others, I now saw my little goldsmith Stokes receiving some friend's goods, whose house itself was burned the day after. We parted at Paul's; he home, and I to Paul's Wharf, where I had appointed a boat to attend me, and took in Mr Carcasse and his brother, whom I met in the street, and carried them below and above bridge too. And again to see the fire, which was now got further, both below and above, and no likelihood of stopping it. Met with the King and Duke of York in their barge, and with them to Queenhithe, and there called Sir Richard Browne to them. Their order was only to pull down houses, apace, and so below bridge at the water-side; but little was or could be done, the fire coming upon them so fast. Good hopes there was of stopping it at the Three Cranes above, and at Buttulph's Wharf below bridge, if care be used; but the wind carries it into the

City, so as we know not, by the water-side, what it do there. River full of lighters and boats taking in goods, and good goods swimming in the water; and only I observed that hardly one lighter or boat in three that had the goods of a house in, but there was a pair of Virginalls* in it. Having seen as much as I could now, I away to White Hall by appointment, and there walked to St James's Park; and there met my wife, and Creed, and Wood, and his wife, and walked to my boat; and there upon the water again, and to the fire up and down, it still encreasing, and the wind great. So near the fire as we could for smoke; and all over the Thames, with one's face in the wind, you were almost burned with a shower of fire-drops. This is very true: so as houses were burned by these drops and flakes of fire, three or four, nay, five or six houses, one from another. When we could endure no more upon the water, we to a little ale-house on the Bankside, over against the Three Cranes, and there staid till it was dark almost, and saw the fire grow; and, as it grew darker, appeared more and more; and in corners and upon steeples, and between churches and houses, as far as we could see up the hill of the City, in a most

* A sort of spinet, so called from young women playing upon it.

horrid, malicious, bloody flame, not like the fine flame of an ordinary fire. Barbary and her husband away before us. We staid till, it being darkish, we saw the fire as only one entire arch of fire from this to the other side the bridge, and in a bow up the hill for an arch of above a mile long: it made me weep to see it. The churches, houses, and all on fire, and flaming at once; and a horrid noise the flames made, and the cracking of houses at their ruine. So home with a sad heart, and there find every body discoursing and lamenting the fire; and poor Tom Hater come with some few of his goods saved out of his house, which was burned upon Fish Street Hill. I invited him to lie at my house, and did receive his goods; but was deceived in his lying there, the news coming every moment of the growth of the fire; so as we were forced to begin to pack up our own goods, and prepare for their removal; and did by moonshine, it being brave, dry, and moonshine and warm weather, carry much of my goods into the garden; and Mr Hater and I did remove my money and iron chests into my cellar, as thinking that the safest place. And got my bags of gold into my office, ready to carry away, and my chief papers of accounts also there, and my tallies into a box by themselves. So great was our fear, as Sir W. Batten hath carts come out of the country to fetch away his goods this night. We did put Mr Hater, poor man! to bed a little; but he got but very little rest, so much noise being in my house, taking down of goods.

3 September 1666

About four o'clock in the morning, my Lady Batten sent me a cart to carry away all my money, and plate, and best things, to Sir W. Rider's, at Bednall Greene, which I did, riding myself in my night-gown, in the cart; and, Lord! to see how the streets and the highways are crowded with people running and riding, and getting of carts at any rate to fetch away things. I find Sir W. Rider tired with being called up all night, and receiving things from several friends. His house full of goods, and much of Sir W. Batten's and Sir W. Pen's. I am eased at my heart to have my treasure so well secured. Then home, and with much ado to find a way, nor any sleep all this night to me nor my poor wife. But then all this day she and I and all my people labouring to get away the rest of our things, and did get Mr Tooker to get me a lighter to take them in, and we did carry them, myself some, over Tower Hill, which was by this time full of people's goods, bringing their goods thither; and down to the lighter, which lay at the next quay, above the Tower

Dock. And here was my neighbour's wife, Mrs——, with her pretty child, and some few of her things, which I did willingly give way to be saved with mine; but there was no passing with any thing through the posten, the crowd was so great. The Duke of York come this day by the office, and spoke to us, and did ride with his guard up and down the City to keep all quiet, he being now General, and having the care of all. This day, Mercer being not at home, but against her mistress's order gone to her mother's, and my wife going thither to speak with W. Hewer, beat her there, and was angry; and her mother saying that she was not a 'prentice girl, to ask leave every time she goes abroad, my wife with good reason was angry; and, when she come home, did bid her be gone again. And so she went away, which troubled me, but yet less than it would, because of the condition we are in, in fear of coming in a little time to being less able to keep one in her quality. At night, lay down a little upon a quilt of W. Hewer's in the office, all my own things being packed up or gone; and, after me, my poor wife did the like, we having fed upon the remains of yesterday's dinner, having no fire nor dishes, nor any opportunity of dressing any thing.

Up by break of day, to get away the remainder of my things; which I did by a lighter at the Iron gate: and my hands so full, that it was the afternoon before we could get them all away. Sir W. Pen and I to the Tower Street, and there met the fire burning, three or four doors beyond Mr Howell's, whose goods, poor man, his trayes, and dishes, shovells, &c., were flung all along Tower Street in the kennels, and people working therewith from one end to the other; the fire coming on in that narrow street, on both sides, with infinite fury. Sir W. Batten not knowing how to remove his wine, did dig a pit in the garden, and laid it in there; and I took the opportunity of laying all the papers of my office that I could not otherwise dispose of. And in the evening Sir W. Pen and I did dig another, and put our wine in it; and I my parmazan cheese, as well as my wine and some other things. The Duke of York was at the office this day, at Sir W. Pen's; but I happened not to be within. This afternoon, sitting melancholy with Sir W. Pen in our garden, and thinking of the certain burning of this office, without extraordinary means, I did propose for the sending up of all our workmen from the Woolwich and Deptford yards, none whereof yet appeared, and to 13 write to Sir W. Coventry to have the Duke of York's permission to pull down houses, rather than lose this office, which would much hinder the King's business. So Sir W. Pen went down this night, in order to the sending them up to-morrow morning; and I wrote to Sir W. Coventry about the business,* but received no answer. This night, Mrs Turner, who, poor woman, was removing her goods all this day, good goods, into the garden, and knows not how to dispose of them, and her husband supped with my wife and me at night, in the office, upon a shoulder of mutton from the cook's without any

* The letter, among the Pepys MSS, was as follows: –

Sir, – The fire is now very neere us, as well on Tower Streete as Fanchurch Street side, and we little hope of our escape but by that remedy, to yᵉ want whereof we doe certainly owe yᵉ loss of yᵉ City, namely, yᵉ pulling down of houses in yᵉ way of yᵉ fire. This way Sir W. Pen and myself have so far concluded upon yᵉ practising, that he is gone to Woolwich and Deptford to supply himself with men and necessarys in order to the doeing thereof; in case, at his returne, our condition be not bettered, and that he meets with his R. Hˢ approbation, which I have thus undertaken to learn of you. Pray please to let me have this night, at whatever hour it is, what his R. Hˢ directions are in this napkin, or any thing, in a sad manner, but were merry. Only now and then, walking into the garden, saw how horribly the sky looks, all on a fire in the night, was enough to put us out of our wits; and, indeed, it was extremely dreadful, for it looks just as if it was at us, and the whole heaven on fire. I after supper walked in the dark down to Tower Street, and there saw it all on fire, at the Trinity House on that side, and the Dolphin Tavern on this side, which was very near us; and the fire with extraordinary vehemence. Now begins the practice of blowing up of houses in Tower Street, those next the Tower, which at first did frighten people more than any thing; but it stopped the fire where it was done, it bringing down the houses to the ground in the same places they stood, and then it was easy to quench what little fire was in it, though it kindled nothing almost. W. Hewer this day went to see how his mother did, and comes last home, telling us how he hath been forced to

particular. Sir J. Minnes and Sir W. Batten having left us, we cannot add, though we are well assured of their, as well as all ye neighbourhood's concurrence.

Y^r obedient Serv^{nt},

S. P.

Sir W. Coventry,

    Septr. 4, 1966.

remove her to Islington, her house in Pye Corner being burned; so that the fire is got so far that way, and to the Old Bayly, and was running down to Fleet Street; and Paul's is burned, and all Cheapside. I wrote to my father this night, but the post-house being burned, the letter could not go.

5 September 1666

I lay down in the office again upon W. Hewer's quilt, being mighty weary, and sore in my feet with going till I was hardly able to stand. About two in the morning my wife calls me up, and tells me of new cryes of fire, it being come to Barking Church, which is the bottom of our lane.* I up; and finding it so, resolved presently to take her away, and did, and took my gold, which was about £2350, W. Hewer and Jane down by Proundy's boat to Woolwich; but, Lord! what a sad sight it was by moonelight, to see the whole City almost on fire, that you might see it as plain at Woolwich; as if you were by it. There, when I come, I find the gates shut, but no guard kept at all; which troubled me, because of discourses now begun, that there is a plot in it, and that the French had done it. I got the gates open, and to Mr Shelden's, where

* Seethings Lane.

I locked up my gold, and charged my wife and W. Hewer never to leave the room without one of them in it, night or day. So back again, by the way seeing my goods well in the lighters at Deptford, and watched well by people. Home, and whereas I expected to have seen our house on fire, it being now about seven o'clock, it was not. But to the fire, and there find greater hopes than I expected; for my confidence of finding our Office on fire was such, that I durst not ask any body how it was with us, till I come and saw it was not burned. But, going to the fire, I find, by the blowing up of houses, and the great help given by the workmen out of the King's yards, sent up by Sir W. Pen, there is a good stop given to it, as well at Marke Lane end as ours; it having only burned the dyall of Barking Church, and part of the porch, and was there quenched. I up to the top of Barking steeple, and there saw the saddest sight of desolation that I ever saw; every where great fires, oyle-cellars, and brimstone, and other things burning. I became afraid to stay there long, and therefore down again as fast as I could, the fire being spread as far as I could see it; and to Sir W. Pen's, and there eat a piece of cold meat, having eaten* nothing

* He forgot the shoulder of mutton from the cook's the day before.

since Sunday, but the remains of Sunday's dinner. Here I met with Mr Young and Whistler; and, having removed all my things, and received good hopes that the fire at our end is stopped, they and I walked into the town, and find Fenchurch Street, Gracious Street, and Lumbard Street all in dust. The Exchange a sad sight, nothing standing there, of all the statues or pillars, but Sir Thomas Gresham's picture in the corner. Into Moorefields, our feet ready to burn, walking through the town among the hot coles, and find that full of people, and poor wretches carrying their goods there, and every body keeping his goods together by themselves; and a great blessing it is to them that it is fair weather for them to keep abroad night and day; drunk there, and paid twopence for a plain penny loaf. Thence homeward, having passed through Cheapside, and Newgate market, all burned; and seen Anthony Joyce's house in fire; and took up, which I keep by me, a piece of glass of the Mercers' chapel in the street, where much more was, so melted and buckled* with the heat of the fire like parchment. I also did see a poor cat taken out of a hole in a chimney, joyning to the wall of the Exchange, with the

* Buckled,' *i.e.* bent; in which sense it is used by Shakespeare, Henry IV., Part II., act i., scene 3.

hair all burned off the body, and yet alive. So home at night, and find there good hopes of saving our office; but great endeavours of watching all night, and having men ready; and so we lodged them in the office, and had drink and bread and cheese for them. And I lay down and slept a good night about midnight: though, when I rose, I heard that there had been a great alarme of French and Dutch being risen, which proved nothing. But it is a strange thing to see how long this time did look since Sunday, having been always full of variety of actions, and little sleep, that it looked like a week or more, and I had forgot almost the day of the week.

6 September 1666

Up about five o'clock, and met Mr Gauden at the gate of the office, I intending to go out, as I used, every now and then, to-day, to see how the fire is, to call our men to Bishop's-gate, where no fire had yet been near, and there is now one broke out: which did give great grounds to people, and to me too, to think that there is some kind of plot in this, on which many by this time have been taken, and it hath been dangerous for any stranger to walk in the streets, but I went with the men, and we did put it out in a little time; so that that was well again. It was pretty to see how hard the women did work in the cannells, sweeping of water; but then they would scold for drink, and be as drunk as devils. I saw good butts of sugar broke open in the streets, and people give and take handsfull out, and put into beer, and drink it. And now all being pretty well, I took boat, and over to South-warke, and took boat on the other side the bridge, and so to Westminster, thinking to shift myself, being all in dirt from top to bottom; but could not there find any place to buy a shirt or a pair of gloves. Westminster Hall being full of people's goods, those in Westminster having removed all their goods, and the Exchequer money put into vessels to carry to Nonsuch;* but to the Swan, and there was trimmed: and then to White Hall, but saw nobody; and so home. A sad sight to see how the river looks: no houses nor church near it, to the Temple, where it stopped. At home, did go with Sir W. Batten, and our neighbour, Knightly, who, with one more, was the only man of any fashion left in all the neighbour-hood thereabouts, they all removing their goods, and leaving their houses to the mercy of the fire; to Sir R. Ford's, and there dined in an earthen platter – a fried

* At which house the Exchequer had been kept, during the
plague.

breast of mutton; a great many of us, but very merry, and indeed as good a meal, though as ugly a one, as ever I had in my life. Thence down to Deptford, and there with great satisfaction landed all my goods at Sir G. Carteret's safe, and nothing missed I could see or hear. This being done to my great content, I home, and to Sir W. Batten's, and there, with Sir R. Ford, Mr Knightly, and one Withers, a professed lying rogue, supped well, and mighty merry, and our fears over. From them to the office, and there slept with the office full of labourers, who talked, and slept, and walked all night long there. But strange it is to see Clothworkers' Hall on fire these three days and nights in one body of flame, it being the cellar full of oyle.

7 September 1666

Up by five o'clock; and, blessed be God! find all well; and by water to Pane's Wharfe. Walked thence, and saw all the towne burned, and a miserable sight of Paul's church, with all the roofs fallen, and the body of the quire fallen into St. Fayth's; Paul's school also, Ludgate, and Fleet Street. My father's house, and the church, and a good part of the Temple the like. So to Creed's lodging, near the New Exchange, and there find him laid down upon a bed; the house all unfurnished, there being fears of the fire's coming to them. There borrowed a shirt of him, and washed. To Sir W. Coventry at St. James's, who lay without curtains, having removed all his goods; as the King at White Hall, and every body had done, and was doing: He hopes we shall have no public distractions upon this fire, which is what every body fears, because of the talk of the French having a hand in it. And it is a proper time for discontents; but all men's minds are full of care to protect themselves and save their goods: the Militia is in arms every where. Our fleetes, he tells me, have been in sight one of another, and most unhappily by fowle weather were parted, to our great loss, as in reason they do conclude; the Dutch being come out only to make a shew, and please their people; but in very bad condition as to stores, victuals, and men. They are at Boulogne, and our fleet come to St. Ellen's. We have got nothing, but have lost one ship, but he knows not what. Thence to the Swan, and there drank; and so home, and find all well. My Lord Brouncker, at Sir W. Batten's, tells us the Generall* is sent for up, to come to advise with the King about business at this juncture, and to keep all quiet; which is great honour to

22   * The Duke of Albemarle.

him, but I am sure is but a piece of dissimulation. So home, and did give orders for my house to be made clean; and then down to Woolwich, and there find all well. Dined, and Mrs Markham come to see my wife. This day our Merchants first met at Gresham College, which, by proclamation, is to be their Exchange. Strange to hear what is bid for houses all up and down here; a friend of Sir W. Rider's having £150 for what he used to let for £40 per annum. Much dispute where the Custome House shall be; thereby the growth of the City again to be foreseen. My Lord Treasurer, they say, and others, would have it at the other end of the town. I home late to Sir W. Pen's, who did give me a bed, but without curtains or hangings, all being down. So here I went the first time into a naked bed, only my drawers on; and did sleep pretty well: but still both sleeping and waking had a fear of fire in my heart, that I took little rest. People do all the world over cry out of the simplicity of my Lord Mayor in generall; and more particularly in this business of the fire, laying it all upon him. A proclamation is come out for markets to be kept at Leadenhall and Mile-end Greene, and several other places about the town; and Tower Hill, and all churches to be set open to receive poor people.

I stopped with Sir G. Carteret to desire him to go with us, and to enquire after money. But the first he cannot do, and the other as little, or says, 'when we can get any, or what shall we do for it?' He, it seems, is employed in the correspondence between the City and the King every day, in settling of things. I find him full of trouble, to think how things will go. I left him, and to St. James's, where we met first at Sir W. Coventry's chamber, and there did what business we could, without any books. Our discourse, as every thing else, was confused. The fleet is at Portsmouth, there staying a wind to carry them to the Downes, or towards Boulogne, where they say the Dutch fleet is gone, and stays. We concluded upon private meetings for a while, not having any money to satisfy any people that may come to us. I bought two eeles upon the Thames, cost me six shillings. Thence with Sir W. Batten to the Cock-pit, whither the Duke of Albemarle is come. It seems the King holds him so necessary at this time, that he hath sent for him, and will keep him here. Indeed, his interest in the City, being acquainted, and his care in keeping things quiet, is reckoned that, wherein he will be very serviceable. We to him: he is courted in appearance by every body. He is very kind to us; and I perceive he lays by all business of the fleet at present, and minds the City, and is now hastening to Gresham College, to discourse with the Aldermen. Sir W. Batten and I home, where met my brother John, come to town to see how things are done with us, and then presently he with me to Gresham College; where infinity of people, partly through novelty to see the new place, and partly to find out and hear what is become one man of another. I met with many people undone, and more that have extraordinary great losses. People speaking their thoughts variously about the beginning of the fire, and the rebuilding of the City. Then to Sir W. Batten's, and took my brother with me, and there dined with a great company of neighbours, and much good discourse; among others, of the low spirits of some rich men in the City, in sparing any encouragement to the poor people that wrought for the saving their houses. Among others, Alderman Starling, a very rich man, without children, the fire at next door to him in our lane, after our men had saved his house, did give 2s. 6d. among thirty of them, and did quarrel with some that would remove the rubbish out of the way of the fire, saying that they come to steal. Sir W. Coventry told me of another this morning in Holborne, which he showed the King: that when it was offered to stop the fire near his house for such a reward that come but to 2s.

6*d*. a man, among the neighbours, he would give but 18*d*. Thence to Bednall Green by coach, my brother with me, and saw all well there, and fetched away my journall-book, to enter for five days past. I was much frighted and kept awake in my bed, by some noise I heard a great while below stairs; and the boys not coming up to me when I knocked. It was by their discovery of some people stealing of some neighbours' wine that lay in vessels in the streets. So to sleep; and all well all night.

9 September 1666

(Sunday.) Up; and was trimmed, and sent my brother to Woolwich to my wife, to dine with her. I to church, where our Parson made a melancholy but good sermon; and many and most in the church cried, specially the women. The church mighty full; but few of fashion, and most strangers. I walked to Bednall Green, and there dined well, but a bad venison pasty, at Sir W. Rider's. Good people they are, and good discourse, and his daughter Middleton a fine woman, discreet. Thence home, and to church again, and there preached Dean Harding;* but, methinks, a bad, poor sermon, though

26   * Nathaniel Hardy, Dean of Rochester.

proper for the time; nor eloquent, in saying at this time that the City is reduced from a large folio to a decimo-tertio. So to my office, there to write down my journall, and take leave of my brother, whom I send back this afternoon, though raining, which it hath not done a good while before. But I had no room or convenience for him here till my house was fitted; but I was very kind to him, and do take very well of him his journey. I did give him 40s, for his pocket, and so, he being gone, and it presently raining, I was troubled for him, though it is good for the fyre. Anon to Sir W. Pen's to bed, and made my boy Tom to read me asleep.

10 September 1666

All the morning clearing our cellars, and breaking in pieces all my old lumber, to make room, and to prevent fire. And then to Sir W. Batten's, and dined; and there hear that Sir W. Rider says that the town is full of the report of the wealth that is in his house, and he would be glad that his friends would provide for the safety of their goods there. This made me get a cart; and thither, and there brought my money all away. Took a hackney-coach myself, the hackney-coaches now standing at Allgate. Much wealth indeed there is at his house. Blessed be God! 27

I got all mine well thence, and lodged it in my office; but vexed to have all the world see it, and with Sir W. Batten, who would have taken away my hands before they were stowed. But by and by comes brother Balty from sea, which I was glad of; and so got him and Mr Tooker, and the boy, to watch with them all in the office all night, while I went down to my wife to Woolwich.

11 September 1666

By water, with my gold, and laid it with the rest in my office. In the evening at Sir W. Pen's, at supper: he in a mad, ridiculous, drunken humour; and it seems there have been some late distances between his lady and him, as my wife tells me. After supper, I home, and with Mr Hater, Gibson,* and Tom alone, got all my chests and money into the further cellar with much pains, but great content to me when done. So very late and weary to bed.

12 September 1666

Up, and with Sir W. Batten and Sir W. Pen to St. James's by water, and there did our usual business with the Duke of York.

28   * Probably Clerk of the Cheque at Deptford in 1688.

13 September 1666

Up, and down to Tower Wharfe; and there, with Balty and labourers from Deptford, did get my goods housed well at home. So down to Deptford again, to fetch the rest, and there eat a bit of dinner at the Globe, with the master of the Bezan with me, while the labourers went to dinner. Here I hear that this poor town do bury still of the plague seven or eight in a day. So to Sir G. Carteret's to work, and there did, to my content, ship off in the Bezan all the rest of my goods, saving my pictures and fine things, that I will bring home in wherrys, when the house is fit to receive them: and so home, and unload them by carts and hands before night, to my exceeding satisfaction: and so, after supper, to bed in my house, the first time I have lain there; and lay with my wife in my old closet upon the ground, and Balty and his wife in the best chamber, upon the ground also.

14 September 1666

Up, and to work, having carpenters come to help in setting up bedsteads and hanging; and at that trade my people and I all the morning, till pressed by publick business to leave them against my will in the afternoon:

and yet I was troubled in being at home, to see all my goods lie up and down the house in a bad condition; and, strange workmen, going to and fro, might take what they would almost. All the afternoon busy; and Sir W. Coventry come to me, and found me, as God would have it, in my office, and people about me setting my papers to rights; and there discoursed about getting an account ready against the Parliament, and thereby did create me infinity of business, and to be done on a sudden; which troubled me: but, however, he being gone, I about it late, and to good purpose. And so home, having this day, also, got my wine out of the ground again, and set it in my cellar; but with great pain to keep the porters that carried it in from observing the money-chests there. This day poor Tom Pepys, the turner, was with me, and Kate Joyce, to bespeak places – one for himself, the other for her husband: she tells me he hath lost £140 per annum, but have seven houses left.

15 September 1666

Captain Cocke says he hath computed that the rents of the houses lost this fire in the City comes to £60,000 per annum; that this will make the Parliament more quiet than otherwise they would have been, and give the King a more ready supply; that the supply must be by excise, as it is in Holland; that the Parliament will see it necessary to carry on the war; that the late storm hindered our beating the Dutch fleet, who were gone out only to satisfy the people, having no business to do but to avoid us; that the French, as late in the year as it is, are coming; that the Dutch are really in bad condition, but that this unhappiness of ours do give them heart: that there was a late difference between my Lord Arlington and Sir W. Coventry about neglect in the latter to send away an express of the other's in time; that it come before the King, and the Duke of York concerned himself in it; but this fire hath stopped it. The Dutch fleet is not gone home, but rather to the North, and so dangerous to our Gottenburgh fleet. That the Parliament is likely to fall foul upon some persons; and, among others, on the Vice-chamberlaine;* though, we both believe, with little ground. That certainly never so great a loss as this was borne so well by citizens in the world; he believing that not one merchant upon the 'Change will break upon it. That he do not apprehend there will be any disturbances in State upon it; for that all men are busy in looking after their own business to

* Sir G. Carteret.

save themselves. He gone, I to finish my letters, and home to bed: and find, to my infinite joy, many rooms clean: and myself and wife lie in our own chamber again. But much terrified in the nights now-a-days with dreams of fire, and falling down of houses.

16 September 1666

At noon with my wife, against her will, all undressed and dirty, dined at Sir W. Pen's, where was all the company of our families in town: but, Lord! so sorry a dinner – venison baked in pans, that the dinner I have had for his lady alone hath been worth four of it.

17 September 1666

Up betimes, and shaved myself after a week's growth: but, Lord! how ugly I was yesterday, and how fine to-day! By water, seeing the City all the way – a sad sight indeed, much fire being still in. Sir W. Coventry was in great pain lest the French fleet should be passed by our fleet, who had notice of them on Saturday, and were preparing to go meet them; but their minds altered, and judged them merchant-men; when, the same day, the Success, Captain Ball, made their whole fleet, and come to Brighthelmstone, and thence at five o'clock after-noon, Saturday, wrote Sir W. Coventry news thereof; so that we do much fear our missing them. Here come in and talked with him Sir Thomas Clifford,* who appears a very fine gentleman, and much set by at Court for his activity in going to sea, and stoutness every where, and stirring up and down.

18 September 1666

It was a sad rainy and tempestuous night. I did my business in the afternoon, in forwarding the settling of my house, very well. Troubled at my wife's hair coming off so much. This day the Parliament met, and adjourned till Friday, when the King will be with them.

19 September 1666

* Eldest son of Hugh Clifford, of Ugbrooke, M.P. for Totness, 1661, and knighted for his conduct in the sea-fight of 1665. After filling several high offices, he was, in 1672, created Baron Clifford, of Chudleigh, and constituted High Treasurer; which place he resigned the following year, a few months before his death.

To St. James's, and did our usual business before the Duke of York; which signified little, our business being only complaints of lack of money. Here I saw a bastard of the late King of Sweden's come to kiss his hands; a mighty modish, French-like gentleman. Thence to White Hall, with Sir W. Batten and Sir W. Pen, to Wilkes's: and there did hear many stories of Sir Henry Wood,* about Lord Norwich drawing a tooth at a health. Another time, he, and Pinchbacke, and Dr Goffe,† now a religious man, Pinchbacke did begin a frolick to drink out of a glass with a toad in it: he did it without harm. Goffe, who knew sacke would kill the toad, called for sack; and, when he saw it dead, says he, 'I will have a quick toad, and will not drink from a dead toad.' By that means, no other being to be found he escaped the health. To Deptford, and got all my pictures put into wherries, and my other fine things, and landed them all very well, and brought them home, and got Symson to set them all up to-night. I and the boy to finish and set up my books and everything else in my house till

* Clerk of the Spicery to Charles I.; and, after the Restoration, Clerk to the Board of Green Cloth.

† Dr Stephen Goffe, Clerk of the Queen's Closet, and her Assistant Confessor.

two in the morning, and then to bed; but mightily troubled, even in my sleep, by missing four or five of my biggest books, Speed's Chronicle and Maps, and the two parts of Waggoner,* and a book of cards. Two little pictures of sea and ships, and a little gilt frame belonging to my plate of the River, I want; but my books do heartily trouble me. Most of my gilt frames are hurt. This day I put on two shirts, the first time this year, and do grow well upon it; so that my disease is nothing but wind.

20 September 1666

The fleet is come into the Downes. Nothing done, nor French fleet seen: we drove all from our anchors. But Sir G. Carteret says news is come that De Ruyter is dead, or very near it, of a hurt in his mouth, upon the discharge of one of his own guns; which put him into a fever, and he likely to die, if not already dead. In the afternoon, out by coach, my wife with me through all the ruins, to show her them, which frets her much, and it is a sad sight, indeed. To the office, to even my journal, and then home.

* Apparently Waghenaer's *Speculum Nauticum*.

21 September 1666

W. Hewer tells me that Sir W. Pen hath a hamper more than his own, which he took for a hamper of bottles of wine, but they were carried into a wine-cellar. I sent for Harry, and he brought me, by and by, my hamper, to my great joy, with the same books I missed, and three more great ones, and I did give him 5s. for his pains. The Parliament meet to-day, and the King to be with them. At the office, about our accounts, which now draw near the time they should be ready, the House having ordered Sir G. Carteret, upon his ordering them, to bring them in on Saturday next. Home, and there, with great pleasure, very late new setting all my books; and now I am in as good condition as I desire to be in all worldly respects. The Lord of Heaven make me thankful, and continue me therein!

22 September 1666

My house is so clean as I never saw it, or any other house, in my life, and every thing in as good condition as ever before the fire; but with about £20 cost, one way or other, besides about £20 charge, in removing my goods, and do not find that I have lost anything but two little pictures of ships and sea, and a little gold frame for one of my sea-cards. My glazier, indeed, is so full of work, that I cannot get him to come to perfect my house. In the afternoon I paid for the two lighters that carried my goods to Deptford, and they cost me £8.

23 September 1666

Mr Wayth and I by water to White Hall, and there at Sir G. Carteret's lodgings Sir W. Coventry met, and we did debate the whole business of our accounts to the Parliament; where it appears to us that the charge of the war from September 1st, 1664, to this Michaelmas, will have been but £3,200,000; and we have paid, in that time, somewhat about £2,200,000; so that we owe above £900,000: but our method of accounting, though it cannot, I believe, be far wide from the mark, yet will not abide a strict examination if the Parliament should be troublesome. Here happened a pretty question of Sir W. Coventry, whether this account of ours will not put my Lord Treasurer to a difficulty to tell what is become of all the money the Parliament have given in this time for the war, which hath amounted to about £4,000,000, which nobody there could answer; but I perceive they did doubt what his answer could be. My wife and I for pleasure to Fox-hall, and there eat and drank, and so back home.

24 September 1666

Up, and down to look for Sir W. Coventry; and at last found him and Sir G. Carteret with the Lord Treasurer at White Hall, consulting how to make up my Lord Treasurer's general account, as well as that of the Navy particularly. Found that Sir G. Carteret had altered his account since he did give me the abstract of it: so all my letter must be writ over again. So to Sir G. Carteret, to speak a little about the alteration; and there, looking over the book Sir G. Carteret intends to deliver to the Parliament of his payments since September 1st, 1664, I find my name the very second for flags, which I had bought for the Navy, of calico, once, about 500 and odd pounds, which vexed me mightily. At last, I concluded of scraping out my name, and putting in Mr Tooker's, which eased me; though the price was such as I should have had glory by. Here I saw my Lady Carteret lately come to town, who, good lady! is mighty kind, and I must make much of her.

25 September 1666

With all my people to get the letter writ over about the
Navy's accounts; and by coach to my Lord Brouncker's,
and got his hand to it; and then to the Parliament House,
and got it signed by the rest, and then delivered it at the
House-door to Sir Philip Warwick; Sir G. Carteret being
gone into the House with his book of accounts under his
arme, to present to the House. With Ned Pickering, who
continues still a lying, bragging coxcomb, telling me
that my Lord Sandwich may thank himself for all his
misfortune; for not suffering him and two or three good
honest fellows more to take them by the throats that
spoke ill of him, and told me how basely Lionell Walden
hath carried himself towards my Lord, by speaking
slightly of him, which I shall remember. All night still
mightily troubled in my sleep, with fire and houses
pulling down.

26 September 1666

By coach home, calling at Bennet's, our late mercer, who
is come into Covent Garden to a fine house, looking
down upon the Exchange; and I perceive many London-
ers every day come; and Mr Pierce hath let his wife's

closet, and the little blind bedchamber, and a garret, to a silk-man for £50 fine, and £30 per annum, and £40 per annum more for dieting the master and two prentices. By Mr Dugdale* I hear the great loss of books in St. Paul's Churchyard, and at their Hall also, which they value at about £150,000; some booksellers being wholly undone, and among others, they say, my poor Kirton. And Mr Crumlum, all his books and household stuff burned: they trusting to St. Fayth's, and, the roof of the church falling, broke the arch down into the lower church, and so all the goods burned. A very great loss. His father† hath lost above £1000 in books; one book newly printed, a Discourse, it seems, of Courts. Here I had the hap to see my Lady Denham: and at night went into the dining-room, and saw several fine ladies; among others, Castlemaine, but chiefly Denham again: and the Duke of York, taking her aside and talking to her in the sight of all the world, all alone; which was strange, and

* John Dugdale, chief gentleman of the chamber to Lord Chancellor Clarendon, and afterwards Windsor Herald. He died in 1700.

† William Dugdale, then Norroy Herlad, nighted in 1676–7, and made Garter King-at-Arms. The work alluded to was the *Origines Juridiciales*.

what I also did not like. Here I met with good Mr Evelyn, who cries out against it, and calls it bickering: for the Duke of York talks a little to her, and then she goes away, and then he follows her again like a dog. He observes that none of the nobility come out of the country at all, to help the King, or comfort him, or prevent commotions at this fire, but do as if the King were nobody: nor ne'er a priest comes to give the King and Court good council, or to comfort the poor people that suffer; but all is dead, nothing of good in any of their minds: he bemoans it, and says he fears more ruin hangs over our heads. My wife tells me she hath bought a gown of 15s. per yard; the same, before her face, my Lady Castlemaine this day bought also, which I seemed vexed for, though I do not grudge it her, but to incline her to have Mercer again. Our business was tendered to the House to-day, and a Committee of the whole House chosen to examine our accounts, and a great many Hotspurs enquiring into it. Sir W. Pen proposes his and my looking out into Scotland about timber, and to use Pett there; for timber will be a good commodity this time of building the City. Our fleet abroad, and the Dutch too, for all we know – the weather very bad, and under the command of an unlucky man, I fear. God bless him, and the fleet under him!

27 September 1666

A very furious blowing night all the night; and my mind still mightily perplexed with dreams, and burning the rest of the town; and waking in much pain for the fleet. I to look out Penny, my tailor, to speak for a cloak and cassock for my brother, who is coming to town: and I will have him in a canonical dress, that he may be the fitter to go abroad with me. To Sir W. Coventry's, and there dined with him and Sir W. Batten, the Lieutenant of the Tower, and Mr Thin, a pretty gentleman, going to Gottenburgh. No news of the fleet yet, but that they went by Dover on the 25th towards the Gun-fleet: but whether the Dutch be yet abroad or no, we hear not. De Ruyter is not dead, but like to do well. Most think that the gross of the French fleet are gone home again.

28 September 1666

Comes the bookbinder to gild the backs of my books. Sir W. Penn broke to me a proposition of his and my joining in a design of fetching timber and deals from Scotland, by the help of Mr Pett upon the place: which, while London is building, will yield good money. I approve it.

29 September 1666

Sir W. Coventry and I find, to our great joy, that the wages, victuals, wear and tear, cast by the medium of the men, will come to above £3,000,000; and that the extraordinaries, which all the world will allow us, will arise to more than will justify the expence we have declared to have been at since the war; viz. £320,000.

30 September 1666

(Lord's-day.) Up, and to church, where I have not been a good while: and there the church infinitely thronged with strangers, since the fire come into our parish; but not one handsome face in all of them, as if, indeed, there was a curse, as Bishop Fuller heretofore said, upon our parish. Here I saw Mercer come into the Church, but she avoided looking up. Home, and a good dinner; and then to have my hair cut against winter close to my head, and then to Church again. A sorry sermon, and away home. This month ends with my mind full of business and concernment how this office will speed with the Parliament, which begins to be mighty severe in the examining our accounts, and the expence of the Navy this war.

1 October 1666

All the morning at the office, getting the list of all the ships and vessels employed since the war, for the Committee of Parliament.

2 October 1666

Sir G. Carteret tells me how our lists are referred to a Sub-committee to consider and examine, and that I am ordered to be there. With Mr Slingsby, of the Tower, who did inform me mightily in several things – among others, that the heightening or lowering of money is only a cheat, and do good to some particular men, which, if I can but remember how, I am now by him fully convinced of. Into the Committee-chamber before the Committee sat, and there heard Birch discourse highly and understandingly about the Navy business, and a proposal made heretofore to form the Navy; but Sir W. Coventry did abundantly answer him, and is a most excellent person. By and by, the Committee met, and appointed me to attend them to-morrow, to examine our lists. This put me into a mighty fear and trouble – they doing it in a very ill-humour, methought. When come home, I to Sir W. Pen's, to his boy, for my book, and there find he hath it not; but delivered it to the door-keeper of the Committee for me. This, added to my former disquiet, made me stark mad, considering all the nakedness of the office lay open, in papers within those covers. But, coming to our rendezvous at the Swan tavern, in King Street, I found they have found the housekeeper, and the book simply locked up in the Court.

3 October 1666

Waked betimes, mightily troubled in mind, and in the most true trouble that I ever was in my life, saving in the business last year of the East India prizes. So up; and, by and by, by eight o'clock comes Birch the first, with the list and books of accounts delivered in. He calls me to work, and there he and I begun; when, by and by, comes Garraway, the first time I ever saw him, and Sir W. Thompson, and Mr Boscawen. They to it, and I did make shift to answer them better than I expected. Sir W. Batten, Lord Brouncker, and W. Pen, come in, but presently went out: and J. Minnes come in, and said two or three words from the purpose but to do hurt; and so away he went also, and left me all the morning with them alone to stand or fall. After dinner to work again, only the Committee and I, till dark night; and it ended with good peace and much seeming satisfaction; but I find them wise and reserved, and instructed to hit all our blots. To White Hall, and there, among the ladies, and saw my Lady Castlemaine never looked so ill, nor Mrs Stewart neither, as in this plain natural dress. I was not pleased with either of them. Find my father and my brother come to town – my father, without my expectation, but glad I am to see him. Home, to set up all my folio books, which are come home gilt on the backs, very handsome to the eye. This night, W. Pen told me W. Batten swears he will have nothing to do with the Privateer, if his son do not go Lieutenant, which angers me and him; but we will be even with him, one way or other.

4 October 1666

Up, and mighty betimes to Sir W. Coventry, to give him an account of yesterday's work, which do give him good content. He did then tell me his speed lately to the House in his own vindication about the report of his selling of places, he having a small occasion offered him by chance; which he did desire, and took, and did it to his content, and, he says, to the House's seeming to approve of it, by their hum. He confesses how long he had done it, and how he desired to have something else: and, since then, he had taken nothing, and challenged all the world. To Sir G. Carteret, and there discoursed much of the want of money, and our being designed for destruction. How the King hath lost his power, by submitting himself to this way of examining his accounts, and is become but as a private man. He says the King is troubled at it, but they talk an entry* shall be made; that it is not to be brought into example; that the King must, if they do not agree presently, make them a courageous speech, which, he says, he may do, the City of London being now burned, and himself master of an army, better than any prince before him. After dinner the bookbinder come, and I sent by him some more books to gild.

5 October 1666

The Sub-committee have made their report to the Grand Committee, and in pretty kind terms. Captain Cocke told me of a wild motion made in the House of Lords by

---

* In the Journals of the House of Commons.

the Duke of Buckingham, for all men that have cheated the King to be declared traitors and felons; and that my Lord Sandwich was named. This had put me into great pain: so the Vice-Chamberlain, who had heard nothing of it, having been all day in the city, away with me to White Hall; and there told me that, upon my Lord Ashly's asking their direction whether, being a peer, he should bring in his accounts to the Commons, which they did give way to, the Duke of Buckingham did move that, for the time to come, what I have written above might be declared by some fuller law than heretofore. Lord Ashly answered, that it was not the fault of present laws, but want of proper [ones]; and the Lord Chancellor said, that a better law he thought might be made: so, the House laughing, did refer it to him to bring in a bill for that purpose. Nobody beginning, I did, and made a current, and, I thought, a good speech, laying open the ill state of the Navy: by the greatness of the debt; greatness of the work to do against next year; the time and materials it would take; and our incapacity, through a total want of money. I had no sooner done, but Prince Rupert rose up, and told the King, in a heat, that whatever the gentleman had said, he had brought home his fleet in as good a condition as ever any fleet was brought home; that twenty boats would be as many as the fleet would want: and all the anchors and cables left in the storm might be taken up again. This arose from my saying, among other things we had to do, that the fleet was come in, – the greatest fleet that ever his Majesty had yet together, and that in as bad condition as the enemy or weather could put it; and, to use Sir W. Pen's words, who is upon the place taking a survey, he dreads the reports he is to receive from the Surveyors of its defects. I therefore did only answer, that I was sorry for his Highness's offence, but that what I said was but the report we received from those entrusted in the fleet to inform us. He muttered and repeated what he had said; and so, after a long silence on all hands, nobody, not so much as the Duke of Albemarle, seconding the Prince, nor taking notice of what he said, we withdrew. I was not a little troubled at this passage, and the more when speaking with Jacke Fenn about it, he told me that the Prince will be asking who this Pepys is, and find him to be a creature of my Lord Sandwich's, and therefore this was done only to disparage him. Anon they broke up, and Sir W. Coventry come out: so I asked his advice. He told me, he had said something to salve it, which was, that his Highness had, he believed, rightly informed the King, that the Fleet is come in good condition to have staid out yet longer, and have fought the enemy, but yet that Mr Pepys his meaning might be that, though in so good condition, if they should come in and lie all the winter, we shall be very loth to send them to sea for another year's service without great repairs. He said it would be no hurt if I went to him, and showed him the report himself brought up from the fleet, where every ship, by the Commander's report, do need more or less, and not to mention more of Sir W. Pen for doing him a mischief. So I said I would, but do not think that all this will redound to my hurt, because the truth of what I said will soon appear. Thence having been informed that, after all this pains, the King hath found out how to supply us with 5 or £6,000, when £100,000 were at this time but absolutely necessary, and we mentioned £50,000. This is every day a greater and greater omen of ruine. God fit us for it! I made my brother, in his cassocke, to say his grace this day, but I like his voice so ill, that I begin to be sorry he hath taken orders.

8 October 1666

Towards noon, by water to Westminster Hall, and there, by several, hear that the Parliament do resolve to do something to retrench Sir G. Carteret's great salary; but cannot hear of any thing bad they can lay to his charge. The House did this day order to be engrossed the Bill against importing Irish cattle: a thing, it seems, carried on by the Western Parliament-men, wholly against the sense of most of the rest of the House; who think, if you do this, you give the Irish again cause to rebel. Mr Pierce says, the Duke of York and Duke of Albemarle do not agree. The Mr Kirton's kinsman, my bookseller, come in my way; and so I am told by him that Mr Kirton is utterly undone, and made 2 or £3,000 worse than nothing, from being worth 7 or £8,000. That the goods laid in the church-yard fired through the windows those in St. Fayth's church; and those coming to the warehouses' doors fired them, and burned all the books and pillars of the church, so as the roof, falling down, broke quite down; which it did not do in the other places of the church, which is alike pillared, which I knew not before; but, being not burned, they stood still. He do believe there is above £150,000 of books burned; all the great booksellers almost undone: not only these, but their warehouses at their Hall and under Christchurch, and elsewhere, being all burned. A great want therefore there will be of books, specially Latin books and foreign books; and, among others, the Polyglottes*

* Bishop Walton's great work, printed a few years before.

and new Bible, which he believes will be presently worth £40 a-piece.

6 October 1666

Up, and, having seen my brother in his cassocke, which I am not the most satisfied in, being doubtfull at this time what courses to have him profess too soon; Sir W. Coventry and I discoursed of our sad condition by want of a Comptroller:* and it was his words, that he believes, besides all the shame and trouble he hath brought on the office, the King had better have given £100,000 than ever have had him there. He did discourse about some of these discontented Parliament-men, and says that Birch is a false rogue: but that Garraway is a man that hath not been well used by the Court, though very stout to death, and hath suffered all that is possible for the King from the beginning. But, discontented as he is, yet never knew a Session of Parliament but that he hath done some good deed for the King before it rose. I told him the passage Cocke told me of – his having begged a brace of bucks of the Lord Arlington for him: and, when it come to him, he sent it

* Sir John Minnes performing the duties inefficiently.

back again. Sir W. Coventry told me, it is much to be pitied that the King should lose the service of a man so able and faithful: and that he ought to be brought over, but that it is always observed, that, by bringing over one discontented man, you raise up three in his room: which is a state lesson I never knew before. But, when others discover your fear, and that discontent procures fear, they will be discontented too, and impose on you. This morning my wife told me of a fine gentlewoman my Lady Pen tells her of, for £20 per annum, that sings, dances, plays on four or five instruments, and many other fine things, which pleases me mightily: and she sent to have her see her, which she did this afternoon, but sings basely, and is a tawdry wench that would take £8 – but [neither] my wife nor I think her fit to come.

7 October 1666

To White Hall, where met by Sir W. Batten and Lord Brouncker, to attend the King and Duke of York at the Cabinet; but nobody had determined what to speak of, but only in general to ask for money. So I was forced immediately to prepare in my mind a method of discoursing. And anon we were called in to the Green Room, where the King, Duke of York, Prince Rupert,

Lord Chancellor, Lord Treasurer, Duke of Albemarle, Sirs G. Carteret, W. Coventry, Morrice. Duke of York is wholly given up to his Lady Denham. The Duke of Albemarle and Prince Rupert do less agree. The King hath yesterday, in Council, declared his resolution of setting a fashion for clothes, which he will never alter. It will be a vest, I know not well how; but it is to teach the nobility thrift, and will do good. By and by comes down from the Committee Sir W. Coventry, and I find him troubled at several things happened this afternoon, which vexes me also; our businesses looking worse and worse, and our work growing on our hands. Time spending, and no money to set any thing in hand with; the end thereof must be speedy ruin. The Dutch insult and have taken off Bruant's head, which they had not dared to do, though found guilty of the fault he did die for, of something of the Prince of Orange's faction, till just now, which speaks more confidence in our being worse than before. Alderman Maynell, I hear, is dead. Thence returned in the dark by coach all alone, full of thoughts of the consequences of this ill complexion of affairs, and how to save the little I have, which, if I can do, I have cause to bless God that I am so well, and shall be well contented to retreat to Brampton, and spend the rest of my days there. So to my office, and finished my

Journal, with resolutions, if God bless me, to apply myself soberly to settle all matters myself, and expect the event of all with comfort.

9 October 1666

To the office, where we sat the first day since the fire, I think. Home, and my uncle Thomas was there, and dined with my brother and I.

10 October 1666

Fast-day for the fire. With Sir W. Batten, by water, to White Hall, and anon had a meeting before the Duke of York, where pretty to see how Sir W. Batten, that carried the surveys of all the fleet with him, to show their ill condition to the Duke of York, when he found the Prince there, did not speak one word, though the meeting was of his asking, for nothing else; and, when I asked him, he told me he knew the Prince too well to anger him, so that he was afraid to do it. Thence with him to Westminster, to the parish church,* where the Parliament-men; and Stillingfleete in the pulpit. So full, no standing there; so he and I to eat herrings at the Dog

* St Margaret's.

Tavern; and then to church again, and there was Mr Frampton in the pulpit, whom they cry up so much, a young man, and of a mighty ready tongue. I heard a little of his sermon, and liked it, but the crowd so great I could not stay. Captain Cocke, who is mighty conversant with Garraway and those people, tells me what they object as to the mal-administration of things as to money. But that they mean well and will do well; but their reckonings are very good, and show great faults, as I will insert here. They say the King hath had towards this war expressly thus much:–

Royal Ayde	£2,450,000
More	1,250,000
Three months' tax given the King by a power of raising a month's tax of £70,000 every year for three years	0,210,000
Customes, out of which the King did promise to pay £240,000, which, for two years, come to	0,480,000
Prizes, which they moderately reckon at	0,300,000
A debt declared by the Navy, by us	0,900,000
	5,590,000
The whole charge of the Navy, as we state it for two years and a month, hath been but	3,200,000
So what has become of all this sum?*	£2,390,000

* The remainder of the receipts.

He and I did bemoan our public condition. He tells me the Duke of Albemarle is under a cloud, and they have a mind at Court to lay him aside. This I know not; but all things are not right with him: and I am glad of it, but sorry for the time. So home to supper, it being my wedding night, but how many years I cannot tell; but my wife says ten.

11 October 1666

Memorandum. I had taken my Journall during the fire, and the disorders following, in loose papers, until this very day, and could not get time to enter them in my book till January 18, in the morning, having made my eyes sore by frequent attempts this winter to do it. But now it is done: for which I thank God! and pray never the like occasion may happen.

Phoenix 60p Paperbacks

History/Biograpy/Travel

The Empire of Rome A.D. 98–190 *Edward Gibbon*
The Prince *Machiavelli*
The Alan Clark Diaries: Thatcher's Fall *Alan Clark*
Churchill: Embattled Hero *Andrew Roberts*
The French Revolution *E.J. Hobsbawm*
Voyage Around the Horn *Joshua Slocum*
The Great Fire of London *Samuel Pepys*
Utopia *Thomas More*
The Holocaust *Paul Johnson*
Tolstoy and History *Isaiah Berlin*

Science and Philosophy

A Guide to Happiness *Epicurus*
Natural Selection *Charles Darwin*
Science, Mind & Cosmos *John Brockman, ed.*
Zarathustra *Friedrich Nietzsche*
God's Utility Function *Richard Dawkins*
Human Origins *Richard Leakey*
Sophie's World: The Greek Philosophers *Jostein Gaarder*
The Rights of Woman *Mary Wollstonecraft*
The Communist Manifesto *Karl Marx & Friedrich Engels*
Birds of Heaven *Ben Okri*

Fiction

Riot at Misri Mandi *Vikram Seth*
The Time Machine *H. G. Wells*
Love in the Night *F. Scott Fitzgerald*

The Murders in the Rue Morgue *Edgar Allan Poe*
The Necklace *Guy de Maupassant*
You Touched Me *D. H. Lawrence*
The Mabinogion *Anon*
Mowgli's Brothers *Rudyard Kipling*
Shancarrig *Maeve Binchy*
A Voyage to Lilliput *Jonathan Swift*

POETRY
Songs of Innocence and Experience *William Blake*
The Eve of Saint Agnes *John Keats*
High Waving Heather *The Brontes*
Sailing to Byzantium *W. B. Yeats*
I Sing the Body Electric *Walt Whitman*
The Ancient Mariner *Samuel Taylor Coleridge*
Intimations of Immortality *William Wordsworth*
Palgrave's Golden Treasury of Love Poems *Francis Palgrave*
Goblin Market *Christina Rossetti*
Fern Hill *Dylan Thomas*

LITERATURE OF PASSION
Don Juan *Lord Byron*
From Bed to Bed *Catullus*
Satyricon *Petronius*
Love Poems *John Donne*
Portrait of a Marriage *Nigel Nicolson*
The Ballad of Reading Gaol *Oscar Wilde*
Love Sonnets *William Shakespeare*
Fanny Hill *John Cleland*
The Sexual Labyrinth (for women) *Alina Reyes*
Close Encounters (for men) *Alina Reyes*